Me and the Dead

KATY EVANS-BUSH was born in New York City and moved to London at the age of nineteen. She lives in Stoke Newington with her three children, and writes the literary blog *Baroque in Hackney*. This is her first full collection.

Me and the Dead

Katy Evans-Bush

CAMBRIDGE

PUBLISHED BY SALT PUBLISHING
Fourth Floor, 2 Tavistock Place, Bloomsbury, London WC1H 9RA United Kingdom

All rights reserved

© Katy Evans-Bush, 2008, 2010

The right of Katy Evans-Bush to be identified as the
author of this work has been asserted by her in accordance
with Section 77 of the Copyright, Designs and Patents Act 1988.

This book is in copyright. Subject to statutory exception
and to provisions of relevant collective licensing agreements,
no reproduction of any part may take place without the written
permission of Salt Publishing.

Salt Publishing 2008
Paperback edition 2010

Printed and bound in the United Kingdom by Lightning Source UK Ltd

Typeset in Swift 9.5 / 13

This book is sold subject to the conditions that it shall not,
by way of trade or otherwise, be lent, re-sold, hired out,
or otherwise circulated without the publisher's prior consent
in any form of binding or cover other than that in which
it is published and without a similar condition including this
condition being imposed on the subsequent purchaser.

ISBN 978 1 84471 421 6 hardback
ISBN 978 1 84471 761 3 paperback

1 3 5 7 9 8 6 4 2

*for Mom & Dad,
Mary & Tom,*

and for Em, Nat & Daisy

Contents

The Only Reader	1
The Bog of Despair	2
Life (a Dream)	4
The Metropolitan Opera	5
As the Sun Sends the Sequins on my Handbag Scattering	6
Here	7
My Dish	8
To My Next Lover	10
Dinosaur Opera	11
East Ten	12
Whereas the Strings	14
The Escape Artists	15
The Electrical Paradox	16
Two Egotists in a Hotel	18
Nero the Beautiful	19
Across the Lake	20
Imitating Life	21
The Raft of the Medusa	22
Così Fan Tutte	23
Dissection of a Split Second	25
Between Two Heroes	28
The Giraffe That Wasn't There (and the Giraffe That Was)	29
An Operation in New York	30
Centre Point	31
Or Something	32
After	33
The Wind	35

Moose: an Adventure in Real Time	36
Fragment	38
The Downs	39
The Cathedral	40
Abney Park Cemetery	43
Scared of Knives	44
The Huge Husband	45
Off	46
Bonfire Nights	48
Your Ghosts	49
Our Passion	50
Sugar Bakers Lane	51
Dream: the Twelve Dancing Princesses	52
In Which the Poet Adopts the Shape of a Swineherd, to Little Avail	53
A Later Letter on Art	54
Me and the Dead	55
The Crash (a Love Letter)	56
The Dive	58
The Cave	59
Pity	60
I See the Hudson River, the Hudson River Sees Me	62
The Life Mask	63
The Brass Doorknob	64
A Crack in the Feeling	65
This is Happening	66
The Master and the Future	68
Notes	69

Acknowledgements

Some of these poems first appeared in the following magazines: *Cimarron Review*, *The Frogmore Papers*, *Limelight* (www.thepoem.co.uk/limelight), *Magma*, *Manhattan Review*, www.nthposition.com, *The Pen Pusher*, *Poetry Salzburg Review*, *The Rialto*, *Rising*, *Stand* and *The Wolf*.

'The Master and the Future' won third prize in the Oxfam Poems for a Better Future competition (2003).

Ten poems in this collection first appeared in the anthology *The Like Of It* (Baring and Rogerson, 2005).

The line 'This is Happening This is Happening This is Happening' comes from 'China', which appears in *The State of the Prisons*, by Sinead Morrissey (Carcanet, 2005).

The lines from Joseph Brodsky come from 'I was born and raised in the Baltic Marshland,' which appears on his *Collected Poems*, Carcanet, 2005.

Michael Donaghy's 'The Incense Contest' appears in *Dances Learned Last Night* (Picador, 2000).

'The Electrical Paradox' and 'A Later Letter on Art' are based on many emails from one person. The words are largely, but not all, his; the way in which they have been put together is mine; many thanks.

This book could never have appeared as it is without the support, at various times, of Julia Casterton, Michael Donaghy, Simon Rees-Roberts, Liane Strauss, Andy Ching, Elizabeth Baines and David Secombe. Thanks are also due to Clive Watkins for his invaluable input on 'The Cathedral'.

The Only Reader

As the book can only fall into temporary hands,
Its spine cracked where one page or another's been favoured
By a boy in love with love or a homesick old man
Till its glue dries up and its stitches disintegrate,
Its leaves falling brown and acidic on someone's floor,
Lines scattered randomly and perhaps thrown on a fire;

As the Canada goose honks serenely, unaware
Of foreign towns below him—as only the sky
Has meanings and tones—where foreign people gaze
Through open doors at his leaf-and-cloud-coloured flight,
And the Amherst woods carried with him as he goes,
And the air momentarily clearer where he was;

As the curator loves the careful strokes of the scribe
But can know nothing of the man himself who lived
A thousand years back, knowing only that he was a man
Temporal like us and who lived for the oblique,
Giving the gold-leaf ascender everything he had
Because there was no other place to offer it;

So we keep dim faith with our craft; so the reader
Pulls in illumination, and I send out my letter:
Dear Being, which art the Emperor of the Empirical,
And hope some electrical current will pick it up
To fly on a lightning-bolt like a rag on a kite-tail
So high on the hill that not even time can reach it,
And there's only the poem itself, and a goose going by.

The Bog of Despair
for Liane Strauss

We'd lunched on Greek salad and coffee
in a place with white walls and a skylight,
and when the guy in the corner's phone
went off in a polyphonic can-can
we laughed without even trying to hide it.

We'd looked in a shop where a scarf
of silk sat waiting for me to buy it,
and walked past a dog in a puddle
of mud, who shook his coat,
but missed us—and we laughed.

The Heath was lovely that day—
the air was full of spring.
We'd walked up a foresty path,
past a rubber hung like a thief on a tree,
full of swag, and we'd laughed and laughed.

We'd walked past the swimming pond
and up the mound of Parliament Hill,
talking about John Keats,
and other people we knew, and the dog,
looking for somewhere to sit, and laughing.

But every bench we came to
was engraved in memory of someone
loved and regretted, young, a child,
and I imagined them sitting there
on the slope, or invisibly playing.

The benches sat on the fat slope
facing the concert that is us:
the blink of Canary Wharf,
the London Eye's diamond necklace.
We read them, and flinched, and laughed.

We turned and started down:
you had to get your kids from school,
and I had a shiny scarf to buy,
and the jeweller's-window view
of London had ceased to be amusing.

Your new shoes from Paris stuck
in the mud, and we laughed: *the Bog
of Despair!* We laughed because
we could feel, behind us, up the hill,
the children watching us.

Life (a Dream)
Scene: the Forest

The room was small and the window was big.
The trees outside brushed green and yellow
on the clear panes and, but for the leaves, no sound
except for a little spaniel.
Bark! Bark! Bark! he remarked, into the glass-silence.

The air blowing in the window was also green.
Then Goldilocks had a dream in which she woke
and saw three bears
standing round her little bed,
gazing down at her with their eyes full of love.

And then an aeroplane puttered over the forest,
round and plump as a picknicking family
with a bag of cakes.

Mama Bear sighed and reached for Baby Bear.
Baby Bear was swelled with joy and Goldilocks
stirred a little but slept on
in the snug bed.
One hand curled round the edge of the counterpane
which was like a leaf.

Fondly the bears watched the sleeping pink child
and her curls, the colour of sunshine, fanned out
neatly on the pillow.
Baby Bear's pillow.

The people in the areoplane looked out
and saw the bears and saw the sleeping girl
and saw her wake and smile
and say to Baby Bear, *what's small is big,*
and heard her say, *your room's a window.*

The Metropolitan Opera

Sometimes, like on a 3D ruler where the disciples
eat, look around, eat, it's there
the way it always has been, its drab red-&-olive plaid
laid out with the perspective of a medievalist,
along the wall. On it the father lies
with head to double-doorway and stockinged feet
to window, elongated like the couch,
his arms folded in saintly repose.

The room looks paler in retrospect
than in fact it was, as if it were a fresco
on crumbling plaster,
while the voices echo even now
of those whose names are spoken
with reverence, but not till after: Sills, Callas
(tragic non-sequitur in this age of faith),
Fischer-Dieskau. It's a play of light
that brings it up, the wintry glow
of 3 p.m. on couchback, on the rough
upholstery's red-&-gold check, thin curtains hanging sheer
against the assaulted glass and outside's
secular grey-&-white; or else a strain of Verdi;
Puccini, who cried like a child in his room
when Mimi died by his own pen;
Bizet, where the honest peasant choir
leads us along till suddenly the beloved
breaks free and soars like a bird above the others,
her voice swirling tempestuously around the house,
and romance smashes in and becomes
the cathedral and everything it touches turns to gold.

As the Sun Sends the Sequins on my Handbag Scattering

a train clacks over a stone bridge.
Inside it, my head's on your chest.
You look, and your hand stops moving;
you look up, your eyes bright, and say:
ah, the lovely Calder! See its currents.
Beneath its grey water the fish swim out, uncaught,
their blue-green resplendence
in curious hidden turns.
As you talk of carboniferous limestone beds
you're dotted with gold specks thrown
by the sun, by my bag.
The bridge flashes past behind us;
banks of azalea wink and are tossed aside.
There was a stab, hard to see
if you so much as blinked, light on water,
perhaps a fin. Who knows what we're beginning.
I feel your muscles flex, and you lean
towards me again.

Here

I hold on tight to the knee-length grass, lowering
one foot and then the other down the chalky path
behind you in my split-toed Japanese-style
city trainers. You're in desert boots, talking.
You pull all the seeds from a stalk with one rapid
pull, laughing, and throw them over your shoulder.
The path cuts through the downs like a jet trail
dropped from an enormous mineral sky.

You tell me: *there's even a kind of beetle that only
lives here, a species of its own — the Whitehawk
Variant* something-or-other. When I ask:
how do they know there isn't a family the same
somewhere in Nepal? You say *there just isn't,
this place is unique.* You ask if I'm okay there,
and I am. Anyway, you're used to rolling rat-arsed
down this hill, then waking next morning bruised,
bed-full of pollen, picking straw from your clothes
after too many pints of cider. Far down
a girl in the playground runs like a droplet.

A giant wood-louse, two snails, a narrow miss,
me slip-footed on the twisty surface.
They're lucky, you say, *I'd have had them for bait
another day!* But they're sedate as a WI lady
and her husband. I move aside and there
another Mr and Mrs emerge from the grass,
northwards, their necks craning gracefully out
under neatly-packed shells, pulsing lightly
with each quarter-inch they cover. Brave little snails,
slightly speckled, like no others anywhere.

My Dish

My dish, you're serenely white
except for your picture, and scalloped
round the edge. Your pearlescence has mostly
been rubbed (or scrubbed) away,

though scattered patches remain,
oily-rainbow-coloured: were you moulded
on a bubble? Was your mother a conch?
If I listen to you what will I hear?

Dish, you're my talisman,
my lucky charm, my incantation, my potion,
my memento mori—that is, of the death of my heart—
you're my past, my future, my darling Valentine.

You arrived as a surprise,
a kind of benediction, given away
impulsively by my friend Helen. What I love
is the medallion image at your bottom,

scratched as it is (by the philistine
fork of the pearlescence-scrubbing person).
While I like to think of some thirties librarian
smoothing her hands over your cool

sides, running a varnished fingertip
over your rim as she pushes up her tortoise-shell
glasses, fidgets, and sighs,
admiring your adherence to the romantic,

it was probably some housewife who did it,
over years of Sunday trifles,
scraping all your sea-gloss with a spoon.
You were her reminder, my dish, my pot,

my little ramekin, of how it was with her
when she was young and loved her husband.
Your picture made me have to have you:
Dante Alighieri's Armageddon, his first

glimpse of Beatrice. I recognised him
instantly by the crashing of his heart
against his body's wall and the thunderstruck
look on his face; Beatrice cool as the foaming brine.

Around them a wisp of lustre curls
like smoke trailing from a campfire,
or something more centrifugal, and past that
the devotional nun's-white of old porcelain.

Dante knew he was smitten,
smote, smattered, smut, smited—
oh my bowl, I'll ignore the obvious rhyme for that
last word—we all know he never got over it.

On you, he leans against a wall, by a canal,
his last moment of casual living
just over; in the clear mediaeval light he looks
like a pillar, a shiny column, a poem.

To My Next Lover

All weekend I kept thinking about you:
as I cleaned the kitchen, changed my bed,
lay in the bath with a book, eyed up a waiter,
tried new perfume on, I thought about you—
bought new underwear—yes, especially then,
about you, looking into the mirror
in the changing room and again at home,
running my hands over lace, undoing clasps
(but only to put on the old ones and wash the windows).

I thought about your eyes across a crowd,
hooking into mine, unclasping mine,
as you come closer, breathing my perfume;
I thought about you while kneeling on the carpet
to reach a fork that was lying under the table;
I thought about you when Sharon on *Eastenders*
got into it with her adopted brother—
smashing all the vases where they fell—
I thought aboutcha then, lover, an' all.

Too long I've had no lover—just the last,
and that's no lover to speak of. I've been loveless,
clasped and virtuous, dreamless, skinless, tongueless:
but now I have you, Next, a leap to the future
tense: I'm thinking about your hips, your weight,
your possibilities, your previous lovers;
and even if it never happens, the kissing
of places beneath new lace, you'll still have been
my next lover, now. Thanks for the weekend.

Dinosaur Opera

> 'There will be a dinosaur opera one day—I'm sure of it!'
> — ROISIN TIERNEY

There *will* be a dinosaur opera one day;
leaf-eaters will roam the stage
and carnivores lift their diaphragms in song.
Good old Pachysephalasaurus will sound
his hollow baritone in hunger
for beauty only, and the pterosaur will soar
for the feeling, not because he has to.

The Museum of Natural History
will lie unopened as its former citizens take up
where the others left off, writing poems,
making TV documentaries and electric cars.
When the great tenor Tyrannosaurus
complains of the smallness of his damask waistcoat
while a small two-leg from costume hovers,
pins in mouth, taking his measure,
the whole notion of extinction will have become infra dig.

The stage at the Opera House will be hung with vines;
mysterious blue-green pools will gleam
in hazy light which will filter through gauzes.
Thunder will rumble, basso profundo.
The woodwinds and strings will warm up slowly
below the ethereal herbivore chorus
polishing up their scales in the wings,
while the audience chitters in its seats,
waiting for the premier of something big.

East Ten
after Catullus X

You can't get more than five feet in this gaff
without running into some bleedin' tosser
Trevor used to do the rounds with.
Today it was this bloke, who just came
back from LA, with a ropy accent
and too much bleach in his hair. I swear
he never stopped looking. Up, down, up,
down: all eyes and no trousers, 'e was.
So Trev, you know what I mean, he's jealous.
You eyein' my bird? Starts winding him up.
Hey Alfie, make much dosh, didja?
But the geezer goes—*you what? I'm loaded,
even my skinflint guv'nor 'ad us
rakin' it in like bleedin' Christmas!*
He's on about a Cadillac.
He says they paid to get it shipped
to a garage in Leyton, he says it's red.
Oh yeah. I'm sick of those randy gits
who think they're flippin' gangsters or summat.
I stare at 'is gold and he stares at my tits,
and Trev can see I'm none too 'appy
so he winks—*all right there, Rod, ya sexy!*
But I've 'ad enough for once, an' I go,
so! you gonna give us a ride?
I push myself right in the guy's face,
smiling sweet. I can feel his breath.
Take us to Walthamstow dogs tonight?
Trev's stressing out but I tug his shirt
and whine like a kid for an ice lolly.
C'mon, be fun, you'll see—ask yer mate!
So Mr LA goes red like his car,
the car 'e don't have, and 'e sputters something
about the garage and payin' 'is tax.
Taxis, more like! I was fit to burst!
The friend stutters something, I don't remember,

walks off swearing, and Trev goes ballistic—
I thought he thought it was funny, like,
but 'e's effin' and blindin' and gives me a slap
right there in the pub! and calls me a useless
cunt! No way am I takin' that crap.
So I slap 'im back, and I guess me ring
caught his earring, you know, it's a real diamond,
and the blood went all over—but it's just a scratch,
and officer, 'e fucking deserved it.

Whereas the Strings

Diligently bows scrape
in the forest of pigtails, alice bands, bandannas;
pink palms hover over the steel pans' dunes, and fingers
finger silver keys behind the front where congas
and other percussives are thumped by beginners.

The teachers keep the tune,
here in the school hall hung with streamers
far out of reach of even the eldest pupils.
There's no piano; there's no saxophone. Studiously
among blond trumpeters, one boy with glasses
plays on a clarinet the depth of a neck-tie:
It's the Muppet Show. A woman in the back
berates her husband for arriving late:
I called your office fifteen minutes ago,
she hisses. *You've missed the strings.*
The teacher on tuba glances at her. Next
the show-off flutes, six older girls with technique,
give us a small andante by Carl Maria
von — von — *Weber* (the tutor prompts),
as well as a piece they wrote themselves, and we
listen and clap . . .
                    whereas
the raggle-taggle strings it was —
bending their faces over polished wood
and working little arms as hard as they could
to keep the pace, but still unable
in their thin decorous eighteenth-century way,
plucking and tapping with bow-ends, remembering chords
while Petra kept the melody on violin,
to compete with the boom unleashed by the boys from Year Two
on samba (they've been practicing at home
in the evenings, on their sisters) — whom we loved.

The Escape Artists

Houdini never told. You asked and asked,
convinced there was some secret. And yet
when he came dripping out of that glass box,
a pile of broken chains on the floor by his feet,
was it not death he'd bit his thumb at?
How you all cheered. You were reborn en masse
in the power-surge of what he'd demonstrated.

But hadn't you spent whole afternoons
helping your children tie up handkerchiefs,
remove jokers, hammer false bottoms—
later looking down, or sideways rather
than at their familiar baby hands only half-concealing
full-sized coins? Ignoring rabbits
poking out of hats, and visible strings?
And what about the tin of sardines
brought from behind an ear? Wasn't that you,
mendacious conjurer? Wasn't that magic?

You don't need a tour of the whale,
its pink sitting rooms and corridors drizzling with damp,
to show you someone lived there
and what they made of it. You've seen the sword
furled in the umbrella stand.
And that metallic plate hanging over your fireplace:
wasn't that once a dragon's scale?

The Electrical Paradox
for RJL

Dear Katie
        (he writes—my second letter this week),
Good news! The problem's solved, I am triumphant!
I'm sure I've mentioned the *hot/neutral reverse*
situation here in my mother-in-law's house.
Well, yesterday, Bob (the painter) started to scrape
the layers in Mother's room—the worst, he says—
which was my cue to start replacing the outlets
and switches in there. I'd already tried to repair
the ancient socket behind her dressing table
three times last year, to no avail, so imagine
my surprise when I uncovered the source of the flux!
Here's how I did it. The radio I plugged in
so I could hear from downstairs when the circuit was off
sounded like it was picking up transmissions
from Mars, though it had worked in its previous outlet.
My outlet tester gave me a reading like nothing
I'd seen before! The whole thing had me flummoxed.
On further investigation the *open ground*
I'd been expecting from previous experience
was really a *hot/ground reverse* in the circuit's run
(which I know to be completely impossible);
all the others were working, and they tested
as *hot/neutral reverse*. However, the *hot*
was connected to neutral in this outlet.
I've put it right; the house now has a clean
electromagnetic field, and I'm vindicated!
On Thursday I fixed Betty-next-door's garage
door, which had jumped its rails (she's also got me
building a deck out back). That wasn't a puzzle
so much as a sequence of routine consternations.
Where it had jumped was a hinge roller unlike the others;
whoever'd replaced them could not get this one off,
and so had left it in place, where it slowly eroded.
I didn't have the option to simply leave it.

Unlike the other guy, I had to fix it.
If I were there I'd take you out for a drink;
enclosed is a picture to give you an idea
of how I'm doing here, which I took myself
by holding the camera at arm's length.

                                          Love, Joey

Two Egotists in a Hotel

Sorry, I'm all over the place. I didn't sleep too well
—the dreams I didn't have are getting insistent in that unlived half-light
where the truth might just unveil itself, and now it's morning.
Am I confusing you? Let's try again, and this time I'll open the curtain.
It's not much sun. There's a couple meandering in the drizzle,
lacking an errand or else their sense of purpose in pursuing it, and a dog,
stray from the looks of it and wet. This old glass pane is distorted
and pockmarked with silver rain; see? But maybe it will clear.
You're pale. Here, look: I'll put the wardrobe door at an angle
so you can see for yourself. The mirror, it seems, exists for me. (You slept
badly too, I'm sure, after all that.) It has no surface, only a depth
which is in fact behind it, and its internal space is outside it, oh please
don't frown. You are the internal which is in fact before it,
and the mirror, without you to perceive yourself on this unlit morning
elbow-propped among yellow blankets, washed-out and annoyed,
backed by that grey window and an unseen ripping noise
of car wheels on wet tarmac, would dissolve into an idea. Right now
it holds you, lightly speckled with splashed dots of someone else's tea
(I hope it's tea) in place between its own hard surface and that other.

Nero the Beautiful

The market hubbub's gone — the town's as still
as the hills that unroll, blue as the linen
that used to hang on a sultry washday
down by the rocks where the slave-girls sang
outside the town. Silent now the vendors,
pickpockets, farmwives — with their rhubarb, rhubarb,
their clank, creak of leather, wheel on cobble,
glug of wine, various gabble — the cat-yowl,
the dog-bark; gone the wishing-well prayers,
the raucous rabble of sailors, the donkey chicken goat
and the hollow enticements of the soothsayers.
Not even a cricket remains to sing of the evening
settling in overhead. Only ash,
dug in around the House of Gold, remains.
Hidden in the hills, its dim silence amplifies
beauty — yes, beauty! — in lines that echo
as if they were music for only the pure of heart,
the immortal… Clouds drift,
rose and amber, through the vast purple
of Apollo's cloak, its wavelengths still untroubled
by jet stream, satellite, white noise, spaceborne debris —
its hem of silence. Listen: a man's sad tenor
ripples and slips into the current, where it floats.
He knows he will be noticed by the gods,
who occupy timeless time, who hear all. Surely
Athene hears him, tilting her goldbraided head,
her gown curling soundlessly over sandals of thin glass.
Of course Jupiter will listen to a man, to a poet,
who has the gift of beauty — unjammed as yet
by any sound not paid for by himself.

Across the Lake
for Pauline

I'm on the deck, you tell me, *looking at Lake Champlain*,
and as you say it I see you standing on wooden slatting,
or maybe leaning on a rail. The sky behind you's in its high American,
shimmering-eggshell mode, bigged-up with reflection.
I also see, kneeling under a pine tree on the lake's far shore,
me—aged eight. I'm arranging three dolls around a rock,
fussing with their accoutrements, their shawls,
pouring lakewater into acorn cups. I ask them,
do they like their rustic sojourn, pine needle cakes,
leaf parasols, birch-paper storybooks? The novel
slurp of the water where it laps the glistening dock?
I could have made a note, folded it up, pitched it across,
to skim the decades, depths. This conversation—
you should write it, send it to where the child I was
is still in the country where you ended up; and somewhere,
where nothing has ever happened, and time is nowhere,
the two notes, meeting each other nose-on, can collide:
an origami swan, question-mark, floating smirk.

Imitating Life
after Andy Goldsworthy

The snowball is hollow. Inside
is nothing and space for everything.
In the print of a painted pixel, that pixel holds
the pupil of your eye, and your eye holds me
as if I were hollow, as if I were a snowball,
as if I were a feather on a canal.
The hollow mouth will hold another mouth.
When the petals of poppies are flattened around a boulder
in a pile of boulders, one boulder can sleep.
It will dream it's a poppy.

We were looking at photographs
of just such petals and boulders. The book
held us like a spell, our thumbs gripped round it
side by side and our hands spread flat under the volume.
My nails were red as a thrill. I said: *the paradox*
of postmodern experience is that it must,
to remain postmodern, remain un-experienced,
or some such flannel. His skin
was smooth as a leaf round a boulder. And then —

∼

Stripped of their quills — picture
my poppy thumbnail on my phone.
I lashed myself to the texts of love as if they were a raft
even while I floated on his kisses,
and the curled red un-experienced leaves
gathered round his postmodern faraway houseboat
in its chill channel.

The Raft of the Medusa
after Géricault

A hundred miles away your boat
still bobbed all night as if you slept,
cradled like the other sleepers
up and down the canal moorings;
lapped at bed level, always moving
but always in the same place in the morning.
The carpet almost undulated
under us, as we sprawled on my sofa
entwined and nearly drunk. I'm not
even sure what we were doing there:
everywhere limbs. We hung on tight
in bed, on carpet, by glassy reflections.
The hardest part was not overbalancing.
You were the one who said it: *what...?*
Across the road the library's flag
went smack on its pole, then painfully billowed.

Cathode-blue on the second night
my cellphone flared: again, again,
fluorescences from a birthday dinner
somewhere else. Slave to the text,
I dropped the phone and you moved my legs
to pick it up: *your friends are like
the raft of Medusa!* Then your phone rang.
We cooked. I had a bath. Your boat
fretted its tether beside the towpath.
Maybe the washing had snapped on its line;
maybe someone looked up for a minute.
I don't know: it was you who said it.

Così Fan Tutte

It was a summer night just made for singing.
The lights up St John's Hill were strung like glass
beads on a necklace, and I limped halfway
up to the late-night shop to get more wine
before I remembered my crutch, my still
half-broken bone springing slightly with each step.
My song, *Fra gli amplessi*, seemed appropriate
to the scene unfolding down in your sweaty kitchen,
foretold two centuries before — a duet,
in pochi istanti, with some staying power
(you liked to brag that you had staying power,
but I don't think that was the kind you meant).
Your nanny was right, the relationship was pathetic.
I'd left you both to fight it out below,
drunk, fighting over me; she thought as much,
thought it was simple, thought she had the right,
her mascara streaked and you ponderously smoking,
darling, you're a bit common you know, admit it.
A bus went up the hill, weightless and bright;
like me it had been up that hill before,
but this time the advert strung along it said:
Admit it. You've been having an affair.
Giungerò del fido amante. What an adventure!
And now this. I could taste the air that night,
the blue-black so refreshing on the naked skin
of my left foot. Somewhere I heard a radio,
a different world. A sudden restaurant light
and a couple drinking under a pleated shade,
hands raised around thin stems, her bracelet gold
in the peach glow as she looked out at me.
Our eyes met and the moment froze. The crystal
set — I mean the set-up — I mean glass coffin —
lurched, and out popped my particular poison.
She looked away and I went on, awake.
The breeze cool after your kitchen, the corner shop

strangely the same. *Sconosciuta*, I think
I talked some nonsense, and I bought the wine.
He handed me my change. It didn't show,
a lui divanti. It was only me.
I turned and started down, still really walking,
in quest'abito bito verrò, by myself,
not missing my gunmetal-grey support,
instead held steady by the net of lights.
Oh che gioia, I have to admit I sort of
got into it. But then, I also knew
from the bathos that she really didn't get it,
battering herself against a man,
il suo bel core, who simply didn't care.
No, of course she did, and she also got,
proverà, her revenge, *nel ravissarmi*!
later on by proving to be pregnant.
Well, that was how it went—but as I told her
when she rang me up next day, still crying,
darling, you know, it's just what people do.

Dissection of a Split Second
for David, who should have been there

Filled with a kind of remorse, she
wishes to issue a formal apology.

Not to him, that would be otiose — no,
to the universe.

No matter how loudly coarse he
is, she never set out to be a terrorist.

She practiced all week and even a year,
in front of her mirror, the art of nonchalance

in the face of the egregious.
But she didn't practice not to look.

So drink tumbles to floor,
knocked by bag or book,

and gin and tonic seep like the tears
of a thousand weeping drunks into red plush,

and crescents of wafery tumbler
rock like cradles under her fingers,

and one laugh rings louder and more true than the others.
One person knows what's gone before.

One person can't resist the satiric pull
of inside knowledge.

When the spine hits his nose he
pulls away blood, and goes

silent. It's *The Corrections* by Jonathan Franzen.
I have to go, he mumbles, and goes.

It weighs at least a pound in hardback,
a hefty dissection of our worm-eaten social codes,

and people are picking it up, feeling it,
laughing, *they'll want this for forensic!*

Checking for specks of the ex's DNA—
but it's clean.

Cubism teaches us life is a prism
and so it proves in moments like this

when the layers and planes are jumbled
with colours and noises which are the same thing,

and he pulls away his fingers redly,
muttering, hunched, and is gone,

and it was the first time she'd seen him
since last March, and then she was crying.

She buys a new drink, she carefully asks
bar staff for a cloth, she mops and pats

the table and the red plush, she
gathers the little cradles,

and all the girls are saying, *well done! That was a long time coming*,
as if it was a train,

but still there's the niggling matter of the universe.
Violence is something she never could endorse. She

laughs even louder than he did.
She didn't mean to show any real feeling,

but from somewhere came a force she
couldn't resist, from her

pitching arm probably, or her heart.
She didn't mean to feel any real feeling:

she meant to be über-cool, of course. She
never meant to throw the book at him.

Between Two Heroes

The day is hot; the trees will be overexposed.
He rushes to the foreground. With his hands
held like pale armbands around the sleeves
of two moustachio'ed old veterans, he smiles,
ignores a hint of menace, and says CHEESE,
in a high-collared jacket that pulls across his chest.
FLASH! A little girl in a white sailor dress
runs past the group. Her concentrated look,
dark hair, dark eyes are like my grandfather's,
and like mine too—but—no ... too soon, too fast,
she looks beyond the frame, not part of this.
He hesitates at first, then meets my eye
with a complicit smile both hard and young:
he still has something of the matinee idol
about him. But listen. He's calling, *here,
here I am*, to me. And behind his smile
I see what I've never seen in him. I see
myself. Across the back of it he's written:
*Chautauqua, 1920. This is me
between a veteran of Gettysburg
and a man who led the Charge of the Light Brigade.*
He's wishing there was more that he could say
—who lived by pulpit, stage-light, tent-light, joke,
by blandishment, by Chinese whisper, by charm,
by tall tale, by excuse, by version, by lie,
by knowledge of mystery, by knowledge of fact,
who was never without a thing to say—
to me—through me, now I'm the exegete.
This was once a humming summer day
with canvas tents, blue sky, a solid child,
two old men in medals, holding their hats,
and a man I know. Oh yes, I know him well.
And now it's taken on a silver sheen
behind which it will gradually retreat.

The Giraffe That Wasn't There (and the Giraffe That Was)

April fool! your father laughed,
hat in hand. You turned and went
back from the window, dragging your feet,
walked away down decades, and into this spot.
Slowly, slowly, everything grew
long as your little face, long as a year,
as long as a sigh, as the downward roll
of a tear or a circus drum, as a giraffe
that grazes on Rochester grass and leaves
just as the lacy curtains twitch.
April fool! your father cried,
after a certain interval:
a rhetorician (look offstage,
behind the curtain, see what lies in the shade—
these vacancies are where the action happens)
whose little trick cast a long shadow
on tricks everywhere: you couldn't get
at a joke without tripping over the fall guy
or over that little girl, shuffling, crying
while her father smiled, shushed, rolled his hatband.
As you tell me the story, a couple of shapes
flit in and out of your picture window,
eating your seeds, vanishing past your curtain;
in here we're dry, but outside everything's dripping.
Later, in a field, a pole
hung with vines that have crept and draped,
with gracey feet and elegant-shouldered neck;
two metal footholds at the top
tilt its face towards the road and us.
It stands and watches, alertly hidden,
jewelled with dew, by a rundown barn
to the left of plate-glass and air-conditioning.
Unnoticed in its green world,
it watches you drive away till you've rounded the bend.

An Operation in New York
for Tom Vink-Lainas

> 'A glance is accustomed to no glance back.'
> — JOSEPH BRODSKY

He went under just before the lights failed. Picture the surgeons, hands flickering, at the precise moment our plane touched down in Newark. 'An incident,' said the captain, and everyone held their breath but no one spoke the words. How the sun glinted off our silver shell! We were like a jewel! But on the ground nothing was working.

Buckets and mops, bad nerves, nothing to drink. Even the toilets were electric. All the machines in the kiosks sat ghosted; bored girls guarded the money in silent tills. Catering trucks were stopped at the gates for fear of explosives. Sat on the floor, we wondered how it was going, while the sky past the plate-glass went pink, then dark, then all we could see was ourselves.

Eventually they let the dinners through. The hospital had emergency power—of course it wasn't so dark. Our second plane slid upwards with the ease of a silvery hand slipping into a glove. Somewhere upstate he slid out of his shell into a lit room. His stitches-in-time were under wraps and the fluid dripped back in.

There is no music like the human voice: 'hence all rhymes'. *I was born in the Baltic marshland.* He said, 'No Russian would write like that' : apparently it's all about the paradigm. I grew up and he sold the Nabokovs . . . I flew away, over and over. 'His heart is fine'. I glinted as I, strapped-up, flew toward islands and lands my olders and betters had left and never looked back.

Centre Point

And when we came out it was so much cooler,
even with the humidity. The streets
were as quiet as after a snowfall, though
my feet felt swollen, and my sandals
thrillingly high and tight.
It was late.
Suddenly you held out a finger: *See,
the tower of Centre Point! the blue
letters, one missing as it must, the way it glows
in the fog, it looks just like a movie!*

I could live in this street, you said,
bringing your line of vision down
to the crooked little place we were, in fact,
in—the ramshackle houses, their stratospheric value
notwithstanding except in that you can't.
Can't live there, that is.
The conversation
oh was about dreams,
about the roof terraces of your imagination,
and then I turned back on the vista that pursued us
down the alleyway,
the CENTRE POIN .
It looked
like a black-&-white photograph,
you agreed. It really could have been noir. I turned
and saw ahead of us two orange flowers
leaning together on a ledge in the dark.
Then we were at your car.

Or Something

You told me the universe is doing something,
I forget what: expanding or flapping
in the wind or something—no matter which,
it's only one infinitely possible universe.
Its only ours and imperfect anyway.
Somewhere somebody else's universe
is either expanding, its particles drawing strangely
away from one another as if in horror but still,
I suppose, part of the pack—
or even shrinking (did we consider that?)
which would be caused by the atoms huddling
close for warmth or comfort
against that flapping wind or something;
rubbing together, the friction,
the blanket of static, creating our electric
storms and other interesting diversions.
The universes are, in their multitudes,
unending and also infinitesimal. Some say
they're parallel while others talk of layering.
Oh, the layered universes—I picture them
piled high like feather beds, the feathers inside them
brushing across each other or something.

After

> 'But how can I describe what happened then?
> Except to say the blind must dream. They smell
> and touch and taste and hear; and you, my dear,
> can dream—are dreaming even now, perhaps—
> while all about you swirls a hidden world
> where memories contend like hungry ghosts.'
> — MICHAEL DONAGHY, *The Incense Contest*

Is it like millions of snowflakes when they fly
past a car window, grey against the black,
the new black that goes forever and the reflection
of a face? Your face? They knock the glass,
lit by other people's headlights,
speeding away out of reach as the car seems to ...?
Or, your letterbox bangs open and a year's post
flies through unopened—will it be like that?
And when you do wake up, what then?
Will it be a chair we'll have to push,
a walking stick, a big Braille book? Or might you lean
rakishly into the camera
wearing an eyepatch and a Panama hat?
Will we read to you on Sundays things you'd had by heart,
will you talk like Groucho Marx, wrapped in a blanket,
calling me the nicknames of other friends?

Where are you now, M, dear? Meandering
in the chasm of your brain like a Christmas flurry?
Or anchored to something infinitely yielding,
like some strand of cosmic mozzarella,
that could go much further than your mental reach
and never snap? Or are you hunkered down,
conserving energy in some upstairs chamber,
working on a mnemonic? Remember that?
Are you fiddling with the radio dial?
Will you catch at indistinguishable words

as they blizzard, backlit, past
the windows of your, windmills of your—?

Mindful of the gulf that yawns and gapes
from husbandry to luck, from earth to heaven,
I know which power will condescend to us
out of season—just so, it's dropped this frost,
and dropped us in it. Here—
we'll try to glean what windfalls we still can—
though we're shivering, and our fingers are numb,
and our baskets have holes, and none of us speak the language,
and we're caught in this snowstorm, sticking out our tongues.

The Wind

Tonight the old willow's down, on the common,
and trains stand useless in gust-whipped sidings.
The Tube's a claustrophobe's darkest suspicions
confirmed—the breath of too many others
and nothing else moving—escaping or trying
to find a way home, but instead
riding the gap-toothed monster
into the maw of danger.

All day, like the unwitting ghosts of ourselves,
dark things we never identified hurtled
past where the sign on the old Horse and Groom
creaked and flapped, and a single red leaf came to rest
through a crack on the windowsill,
curling its tip to the room.

Moose: an Adventure in Real Time
for JS & all the gang

I trawled the web a lot, these unquiet months.
My wrist twinged like a played-out bungee
but not one word shook loose:
it was me or my mouse. Then,
one wintry night, I googled a certain
screen-door slam—some kitchen table, dad-in-hat,
always-summer never-scene I don't remember—
Leave it to Beaver . . . but no,
you can't go back.
              So,
abandoning the lugubrious lagoon
of porn I found instead, and recalling
your home truth (*there are no reruns*),
I typed in *Northern Exposure*.

⁓

My DVD amuses you when I hand it,
like homework, over the breakfast bar:
ten episodes, one monologue, a pixelated
printout of the trebuchet
                      (*'it's not
about the thing you fling, it's the fling itself'*),
a present-in-past-in-present present
            from me to us; but I couldn't get the moose.

⁓

We're nearly all here, still, and remorseless
January moves over us with its impenetrable viz,
                        which we ignore,
spooning our chocolate mousse, and laugh
nostalgically about the toaster oven:
its tailfin schoolbus quarterback shoulders,
its promise. I lean and watch

silver flashes flashing spoon-to-mouth, suddenly stuck
                     for ideas (or is it words)
as the monstrous dusk
flings itself over windows, shrouding the train lines,
all but their random Morse code
glinting along the points, past us,
        who search one another with keen eyes . . .

~

        . . . and in Alaska,
a lost world far from our toaster oven
and the kitchen-top with its comfortable fruit platter and CD-
    box,
                        a moose,
a wild moose is roaming with no concept of time
or of life or of death, pointlessly looking
this way and that in some nature-ridden forest,
not even getting into town like in *Northern Exposure*,
        and oh, so much more morose than us,
my Muses.

Fragment
after Sappho

You've packed more into the years, you tell me
across the table. You look straight into my gaze but your eyes
are somehow empty, and dark circles whorl around them
almost energetically until you seem to lose
tone, or shape, and you come to have no eyes at all,
or not your own eyes anyway, because
although I can clearly see something there
it's as if your suitcase is sitting in the hall, packed,
and the driver looks in at the door
not really expecting a tip, and your mouth
is awkward, too, not knowing how to sit,
and I realise you have completely
effaced yourself. I sip my sauvignon blanc.
Elbows on the table, you palm
your hands together. I watch them disappear:
your fingers, delicate and white
to begin with, taper
to nothing, eventually. They can do nothing.
And across the table

The Downs

Who knows how many
layers on layers on layers?
Everywhere! How many
mounds became hills
before they became
history, names, places?
We sometimes recognise
their scraps, their shoes . . .
How many of them,
long-haired, brown-eyed,
fond of a story, still
maybe almost warm,
were carted, shouldered,
leather-stretchered, wheel-
jolted to where
only bones can survive?
Tell me what kind
of love was that?
To build the earth?
Their poor heads, bowed
in sadness, yes,
sackcloth-hooded,
knowing the future!
Even down below us
their roads persist, rutted
with procession, recession,
procession. How much
smaller their world
must have been:
how much taller we
can stand, so cool, so
further from the fire.

The Cathedral

Bells, like voices, open round and clear.
Like life they'll paralyse you with their din.
Like steel cables they tense and draw you in.
They ring what you don't think you want to hear.

~

Is this noise the call to God? No: church,
the daily manifest, the nuthouse scrawl
we proffer in the face of the sublime,
sublime itself our febrile definition
of what is re-created in the jangle
of those bells.
              Now, see from this perspective:
a cobbled yard, its cracks grown through with grass,
set with chairs and tables, set with girls
in after-work groups drinking Chardonnay,
five feet lower than the Cathedral's ground.
Hidden at elbow-level in the earth
lie our silent companions—monks and priests
now rotted to bone, a millennium deeper in.
We sit in the street of a city they'd forgotten,
except for the Latin of their liturgy:
that old hub of the wheel, Londinium.

This flattening out's an oversimplification,
of course, when everything's built on what's before:
power, money, plumbing, so. We rest
deracinated (or maybe happiness
is just a diplomatic sacrifice
in the right temple). This place ran like clockwork—
all that logic! All those healthy bodies!
But days went by no slower and no faster
than what came *post* or *ante*; ladies loved
exotic colours, geometric things;

and then the legion Romans went away,
leaving behind—well—what was left of us.

And what was there for the office girls after that?
Religion without reason? Mystery
unasked, explained—a renaissance for the fairies—
a petty, personal, unechoed heaven?
In those days vines choked other vines on banks
where mosaic hearth-tiles dulled, cracked, sank.
Forgotten bones worked loose in dead soil.
But things persist involuntarily.
Even in the years of what's been told—
spread eagles on the beaches, burning thatch,
blood-red sunsets auguring dark mornings—
slowly, somehow, in those centuries
the earth itself grew larger anyway
till every man stood higher than before.

The clappers clash in carefree summer air.
Above this wine bar, mediaeval ground
asserts what it was made for building on—
a principle of light (*let there be light*).
The thing that can't be known lies deeper now
but reaches us on soundwaves set up then.
In those days the Virgin's azurite
shone over daily plainsong; girls and women
passed through doors where light streamed in above
from windows shaped like roses, fold on fold.
Schools were founded, libraries were opened,
and the whole creaking horsecart of civilisation
jerked into motion again.
                                  And here I sit,
after all that, with a crisp sauvignon blanc,
tracing the runnels formed along my glass
while level with my head the old foundations

strain to hold the towers up over the yard
in their joyful confusion.
Giotto couldn't have painted it more like this:
jostling planes of nave, choir, vestry, roofs,
the rectangles smoothed to seven kinds of cream,
pennants, downpipes, buttresses; gothic arches
topped with clusters of faces—kings, or bishops
smiling with a vague, impersonal love.

By love and coloured windows, *light from light*,
by excellence and exuberance, both, we come
nearer to what God wants from us.
                                Where I sit
the bells' rapturous clamour is a challenge:
it crashes down on me like falling stone
to make me try to build myself again.

∼

God. Love of God. Love. What we apprehend
or grasp is slight. This building is a stave
in three dimensions (which are all we have)
of the larger song. A single note. Bells end.

A glassy silence. So many people here!
Caught up by cathedral, commute, bridge,
they wander from the bus stop to the edge
and lean out into bruised and tender air.

Abney Park Cemetery

Past, behind the fog,
   beneath, beyond: an old world
     waits, marked out for us.

Its dull heavy stones
   sit, as they have always sat.
     They're in no hurry:

the dead will always be
   dead. They hide their angel heads.
     This is their element.

They lift up to us
   tangles of living holly
     on, between, despite

their stones. Does it drag
   at them, or do they drag at it
     with their hidden bones?

The pavement's crowded
   with shoppers' odd, livid notes —
     a child's orange coat —

each of us a ghost
   in the fog; our hidden hands
     carry deadweight bags.

Merry: to them all.
   Merry Christmas, they mouth back
     in the still grey-black.

Scared of Knives

I've heard that a person who fears the knife,
if forced to pick one up, will lift it
gingerly, with thumb and forefinger.
The blade hangs down. The wrist is limp.
The palm's an open parachute
to float the knife to a safe landing
far away from the field of battle.
The hand must not grip the knife nor ram it
home in the wife, the child, the husband,
the roast joint steaming on the table.

This urge in us is strong: we've seen
the fingers trembling. We've watched a crack
travel the teacup where the tea—
thinner than blood, thicker than water—
swirls its shimmering, doomed surface.
We've plunged a steel blade into butter
and seen the gore inside the jam;
we've watched as serrated silver tongs
dropped, with their ancient pincer action,
a cube. We've relished its dissolution.

The Huge Husband
after Frida Kahlo

The cellophane blocks the light. During the bright hours
the picture itself is invisible: Frida stands
in her own dark and stares straight at her wedding.
But when the shadows come you see
a benediction of doves over her head,
clutching a dirty-pink ribbon. In her emerald dress
and ruby shawl she's exotica made folklore,
and her brows are a child's birdwing.
Beside her stands Diego, benevolent
as the circling doves, holding the palette and brushes
of his greatness, his hand on about a level
with her tightly-wrapped hair. His garments are plain,
honest, working garments. He is the huge husband.
You can't take your eyes off her.

Off

I read about *blinding*
hand-to-hand combat in a sandstorm,
off-stage: *700 Iraqi soldiers killed,*
wrapped in cloth, gritted yellow,
unnamed by the messenger.

Here, unseasonable weather
fixes us like a gel
under leaves not yet engaged,
a vague particle glimmer.
I tried to avoid the papers,
still dazed by dreams
drenched in ineffable colour:

a tearing of silk—I mean, silk torn
as if from a bolt, with a swift rip—
into strips to make a silk-grass skirt
(to wear? for whom?
you're there, but unseeing, unseen);
a bed, its sheets streaked:
something organic in the crumple,
someone fled;

something about a house I couldn't catch,
the basement, all prospective,
a door opened by another hand
and an old man
looking up at us from a silk-swathed table;
a shoeless search in someone's moving sights
down the night pavements
which dissolve into day
like fizz in a glass,

tipping me into this pavement café
where unaccustomed spring
fingers me through the holes in my fishnet tights,
dragging me into its eddy;
I swirl the froth in my cup, thinking,
and I can't hear the cars for the quiet.

Bonfire Nights

I heard they had Justine and Jon
(she's pregnant again) and her son Zed,
and Aimée with her parents and her brother.
The box of fireworks was apparently bigger than ever,
spilling over the top.
The kids said it was great, despite the state of the garden:
more space for rockets, the old sizzle and crack
set up against a pink sky while they all ran around
with sparklers underneath. Two burned their hands.
They had a bonfire too, of course:
this time he set on fire some chair he didn't want.
About four years ago it was our old bed.
Once, I remember, I was standing by myself
out at the back by the dry, empty greenhouse
with its broken panes, while the biggest fire we ever had
raged. The garden was black and strange
with pale shapes around its edges
which were my camellias, roses, peonies.
A catherine wheel was nailed to the hawthorn tree.
Ranged on the wall a row of Jack-o-lanterns,
carved for Halloween, watched.
The air was thick with gunpowder and smoke
and the children were all a bit overexcited, eating sausages,
and every time a bang went the baby cried.
I turned toward the house and looked:
all the windows were a frantic orange, red,
outlined by the black brick silhouette.
It was like those reconstructions of the Great Fire of London,
where you queue and go through the tour
and witness for yourself the lifelike devastation,
and what you notice most is the creepy light,
and the lack of sirens, and a voice-over tells you
how, surprisingly, only six people died.

Your Ghosts

A little one bounces
a ball on the stairs
and never comes back.
The angry one throws plates
and turns off lights.
One woman's a mist.
Sometimes you see them
before you look,
moonlight by the window.
The one with an iron
goes up in a hiss.
Another one gossips in a blue coat.
Sometimes they come
all at once so you can't see
anything else.
One comes at the bottom of a pool
with her three daughters,
identical, looking at you.
A man in a satin coat
and a clear fur hat
stands by your bed.
A green girl walks through the room
slowly, so slowly,
wearing last year's clothes.
One touches your shoulder
under the crucifix and asks,
you all right?
This one leers in the doorway:
don't even think about me.
But you already do.

Our Passion

The doe her buck, the bitch her dog, the cow
a bull or two to pull in earthly favour,

each girl a boy, each crone some wizened geezer:
it's like for like, each skin for its own skin chosen.

And when the skin's done, what falls in between?
When neither cow nor bitch nor girl nor crone,

when likeness' likeness isn't for the choosing,
earth still exacts a choice, requires its flesh.

But look here: underneath the carapace
of skin, in each its own condition, kissing,

torchlight lights our red-cloaked silhouettes
of bone, capillary and empty space;

and what you see is not a choice, but living:
the ghost locked in its fellow-ghost's embrace.

Sugar Bakers Lane

In Sugar Bakers Lane
they strain at fastenings;
the doorways are crooked
under an inverse weight
of futures compressed
and history constrained,
the *now* unbracketed:
tongue, sticky hand,
clove-hot breathing,
skin sweet as marzipan.
A motorbike man,
buckled under leathers;
women and guys
in pinstripes, tweeds, scarves,
look away, press on.
Torn stockings on the brain,
our shagger-beggars—
choosers on a binge,
wishing, not riding—
fumbling on the hinge,
lintel, threshold, cusp, clasp,
their backs against the bins,
confoundedly they sing
and the hand comes up with nothing.
Stories, meanwhile, tumble
like a pound of feathers:
they half-fall, half-fly,
tremble in broken doorways,
confess little things.
We'll fall where we lie.

Dream: the Twelve Dancing Princesses

There are several options.
                         One: the woods
are dark. The mist rolls round the trunks of trees.
You can't see any stars. Through leaves, the sky
is black in tiny patches. You can't see
the babies lying hidden in their baskets.
Wolf-food.
              Two: the lake is black and deep,
cold as obsidian, with ripples like breaks. Night
has fallen but the murky light's unreal,
and the lake might be a swimming pool
for all the nature there. You are surrounded
by high blank walls. Everywhere babies wail.
No; they don't make a sound. They are suspended
on the water like lily pads. You must save them.
A girl with plaits rows by in a rickety boat,
blue, with oars like matchsticks. Out to sea.
It's hard to be everywhere at once.
                                Three:

In Which the Poet Adopts the Shape of a Swineherd, to Little Avail

I love you the more because you remind me
of a painting I saw, of a young pig

kneeling to declare its love to a swineherd.
Oh love me not, young swineherd-fancier,

keening at the morning star, staring at my—
leave me, pig-headed swine that I too am.

Desiring to be heard, and panting
with the effort of the hill, the still-

reeling porcine lover prepares its declaration,
fated always to be ill-fêted.

For why should all my originality,
my selfness (or anyone's) be subsumed

in some porkish hankering to be loved,
to be not part of the herd, to hoard goodwill

like a memento—nailing its pictures to your hard-walled heart
—hoping that through accumulation,

by laying its platitudes over each other
one by one, its will will supercede will and become

love? The hill declines. The pig becomes a boy.
The swineherd changes back into a girl.

Love becomes a painting with tiny brushstrokes.
The painting becomes a dream I dreamed

long before I knew or thought of you.
The very thought's a vapour.

A Later Letter on Art
For RJL

... and the artists I met were so technique I could not
stomach them. I was happy enough
washing dishes, establishing slowly my iron rule
over the kitchen at Timothy's on Zion St.
(I once sent you a picture, in which I wore
a yellow shirt and held a dishrag, remember?),
playing with colour and texture and building
an understanding of what is relative
or subjective, by living as an artwork.
Spending a life with one person—being one
when you are two—is that not a sublimely evocative
construct? Is that not art?
You wanted to feed me. Oh, let's not even go there,
just let me have a kiss to taste for the next couple of years.

Me and the Dead

Safe in the past where nothing more can happen to them,
they occupy your streets and your favourite buildings
in their ribbons and wigs and silver-buckled shoes.
You often look at pictures of them: they were
more beautiful than the people you know, so serene
in the bright clear colours of the past, with intelligent eyes.
You feel a kinship with them. Reading their letters again
you want more, more. You prowl their houses; run your hand
lightly along the wood, leaning on their door-jambs:
door-jambs with a quaint look, that to them were modern.

Even the dead you knew, the dead you made love to
and will never kiss again, as you'll never kiss me again.
Your past's a rag-bag of scraps jumbled together
in a terrible hurry, it all happened so fast, and torn
from the strain of pretending to go on
when you were the only one in the room still living.
Once, in the still-life galleries at Tate Modern
you stopped by the plastic torso of a woman
filled with shaving brushes held in resin—some blue-striped,
some red and chipped, some grimy from being used
over and over. So much suspended in its clear, yellowed skin.

At first I didn't believe it. Life beats
like jungle drums, it drips, it sweats out, it swarms
like hornets after the rain, and I thought you were mourning
along a natural course like a river-bed, love
boiling up in you waiting to burst forth in its proper season.
I worried that you were unhappy, I wondered what would happen.
I saw only the future, thinking I could be escorted there
by people in crinolines. Only gradually did I realise
you were an assemblage of fragments. That night when you looked at me
and said, *I'm Death, you know*, like something off a '70s album cover,
I still didn't get it. But now I do. Here endeth the lesson.

The Crash (a Love Letter)

When you get to the pub you're already drunk—
You've been down the Old Globe or somewhere
Since lunchtime, and when you come in
You throw your phone down on the table
And start by picking a fight with Jan.
You're questioning my eye-witness account
Of a crash that happened outside the office—
A man just gunned his car at the railing,
Right into someone—and not by accident—
And subsequent riot (this very statement
I note the police believed outright,
And even wrote it down), while you breathe
All over me, and fondle my arm.
You drawl, *I'm playing the devil's advocate.*

As if he needs one. You go to the bar
And Jan says, *I've never seen such rudeness!*
She's laughing: *what a dickhead, man!*
And there was me, trying to soften the rumours.
You bring some drinks and then your phone
Starts to play *the Ride of the Valkyries;*
Next thing I know you're out on the pavement,
Pacing it flat, like a pent-up tiger
Over the limit, for ten minutes.
I know you're talking to her. Finally
You come back in and start to try
To engage our attention but it's too late.
Jan says, *I can't take any more of this shit!*
And leaves with a single toss of the silk
Hydrangea she keeps in the back of her hair.
What's her problem? you say, five times,
Leaning on me, gripping my arm.

Next morning you wake me at 7.15
Beginning a half-hour fight on the phone

With the woman who uses her child as a pawn.
I've heard it before. I listen at first
From the top of the stairs, but then I get bored
And go back to bed. But I leave before 8.
Well, you get off the phone and ask me to go.
That's your greatest character trait,
You always say—you're straight as a die.
You kiss me—as always, perfunctory, dry—
So then I walk the two miles to work,
Which gives me time to think—and you know,
I kind of wish things were different.
I'm fishing around for my keys in my bag
When I notice the bloodstains still on the pavement.

The Dive
i.m. ML

Just last week we swam in my mother's pool,
your brother and I—he wore some white cutoffs
he'd quickly made by the car when he arrived,
(cutting his fingertip along with his jeans).
He sat on the edge of the pool with the sun behind him,
and we laughed, and he swam with the ease of a porpoise
and looked down the top of my bathing suit a lot.
We talked about you. You'd suddenly come to stay
at your dad's house, with your kids—claimed all the beds—
which meant he had to drive back to New Jersey
that evening, and I couldn't see him next day.

It was the ragged edges that threw me: hacked
with his pen-knife even though there were scissors inside—
more self-sufficient than he had to be—
but on the whole endearing in their roughness,
expressing his eagerness to swim with me.
Anyway, the finesse of his dive lent elegance
to his appearance. Surfacing on the other side
like Superman, parting the water, smoothing his hair,
he dropped ripples of sunlight back on the pool.
The Band-Aid on his finger got wet and came off,
and he showed me the blood, embarrassed, and stuck it back.

Only a week! I'm back under London cloud,
three thousand miles from where you've shot yourself.
But here's my souvenir of you, Marcel:
your brother, cut out like a miracle
in blue and white, the day we slagged you off,
laughing, wishing we had more time. I hoped
I'd see you—a drink, for the old days—not like this,
in my mind's eye, in a pool of your own making.
It's more than regret. I'm holding a terrible weight,
as if that sunlit dive had failed and your brother
was trying to swim so deep the water could crush him.

The Cave
i.m. ML

The falling's the thing: not the final
tumble, when you head-hard the ground,
bullet-holed, rope-cut, bed-dragged,
dredged-up-drowned; it's the stumble, the blip
in your inner ear, the balance-wrecked
moment when tumbling's your any-road to grace
you have to watch or, moment-missing, slip.
The thing to avoid was that: your patient
schlepping-past of junctions, shouldering off
the better-mapped-out options while the path
sloped narrower and narrowed to a drop
into vertical thought, tunnelling downward
where overgrowing vines said eat me, drink me,
shoot me, if you have the bottle; and only
recognised one thing in your hurtling sights,
and that the closer-growing rocky bottom.

It's worse not having a note. I imagine
accretion over the years, a *dripping: dripping*
existence on your surface, mineral build-up
of resistant substances onto what was soft,
e.g., your heart, till you were only stalactite,
pulsing falsely, stone-faced, stuck in your tracks,
till one day you had it—but it was the cave's answer.
Let's pretend for a minute that you'd lived.
Let's leave the cave—come walk with me awhile
underneath the pinhole-punctured sky,
night-silent now. Your hand grows warm in mine.
You see those constellations? Answers come
from questions: listen now and you can hear them.
Thy life's a miracle. Speak yet again.

Pity

Later that evening, unable to sleep, she hears voices:
her father and his new friend, the one they're spending the week with.
Her cunning bed is tucked in a minstrels' gallery over the den.
You've heard of 'playing to the gallery.'
If she turns the light on to read they'll know she's awake,
so she lies there in the lake-dark, listening to crickets
and the low hum of talk she can make out the edges of,
but which does not reach up to her.
Sister and brother are sleeping somewhere in a real room.
At some point everything turns, and she thinks she knows
what she will see if she looks over the panelled gallery,
even though she could not possibly know what she would see.
She looks and what she sees is her father's friend
stretched full length on the summer couch, and her father
curled on the floor with his head on the friend's chest,
with his arm around his friend and his wrist placed just so,
and they are lying there murmuring as peacefully
as a stream running through a shallow rocky place with the sun overhead
The light falls around them. She can feel the love
from all the way up in her cunning bed in the gallery.
She misses her mother.

They've come to this unprecedented cabin in the woods:
the girl, her sister and brother, her father and her father's new friend.
The new friend hasn't brought his kids with him.
There are trees; there is a pier; there are checked blankets
and screened-in porches and things that bite.
One day in the woods the girl and her father walk and stop
and talk; with her heightened awareness she perceives
that it's the first time in ages and feels in herself
the requisite lurch. The birches and pines
form a ceiling, green and dark, and her father begins to sing.
It's the old lullaby she remembers from the long-ago days
which are now under the lake of her childhood;
his baritone slips occasionally to a tenor,

and the tune is slightly off where the notes wander flat or sharp.
And as she stands in her shorts and her halter top
in the dappled light where her tan doesn't show,
it all forms a kind of unbearable, unfathomable depth,
and her eyes sting with tears which she conceals from her singing father.

I'm a poor little lamb who has lost his way, baa, baa, baa . . .
We're little black sheep who have gone astray, baa, baa, baa . . .
This line she forgets but it rhymes with Me,
Damned from here to eternity,
God have mercy on such as we, baa, baa, baa . . .

I See the Hudson River, the Hudson River Sees Me

Woodstock, Red Hook,
Hudson, Hurley,
Shokan, Millerton,
Bearsville, Rhinebeck.

Lake Hill, Peekskill,
Rome, Big Indian,
Kingston, Red Hook,
Tinker St, Marbletown.

Red Hook, Esopus,
Pine Plains, Hudson,
Boiceville, Black Alder
Drive, Shandaken.

Ashokan Reservoir,
Phoenicia, New Paltz,
Zena Rd, Woodstock,
West Hurley Post Office.

The diner in Canaan,
Over the river, Kingston.
Bearsville, Shokan,
Hudson, Hudson.

The Life Mask
Keats, 1816

They think you were dead, John! But you were just patiently waiting
—facemasked in plaster—with eyes closed, for someone to tap it
and cheerfully tell you *that's it! You can get up and talk now!*
Your jaw's clenched to stop you from laughing, or letting ideas
become exclamation—it's all in your temples, the effort,
and also a certain excitement—while Haydon, your sculptor,
admonishes you to keep still or you'll die without cracking
that old childhood mystery: *how do I look with my eyes shut?*
The turban he's wrapped round your hairline, to keep it from pulling—
he'd never have done that if this were a death mask, no need to.
And your eyes, even shut in cold plaster, are so nearly twitching
you no more look dead than the way people look when they're hiding,
peeking behind their hands, counting out—*ready or nothing*—
and someone hears breathing and opens the curtain, and finds them.

The Brass Doorknob

> When ('alas!') I held it to the light, and you
> asked what I saw, I couldn't tell. Nobody knew.

I can't help thinking as you meet my hand
of all I've put my palm against and not dared —

and of all the rooms behind them that I never tried
— the lives unlived and, even more, the deaths un-died.

You give a shock. So still and cool you are.

But what of those I've ventured? (Every door
once opened shows the future — or the past
the present is the minute the threshold's crossed.)

The light behind me's on you like a scar.
The scar is like an Alice band, or star

or galaxy to light your yellow face
with some cold light, some sickle coup-de-grace

reflecting what I hadn't seen. It is
what I don't know if you don't know the words.

This yellowness, this silentness — they lie
across your mystery — our mystery — on my

familiar hand, placed on this ordinary door
that is your message, word and messenger.

A Crack in the Feeling

Broken in their box, quotidian eggs
—date-stamped, unusable. The omelette's off.

An ostrich-egg-in-dome, and plastic grass.
A dino egg, the raptors not drawn right.
These keepsakes can be lifted out of what
was meant to be (that bursting universe).
The robin, just a colour-sample (say
robin's-egg blue, a can of paint): I never
see them lying cracked upon a path,
it seems too much to hope for now.
                                 I like
your eggs arranged in circles on the ground
(the largest first, then smaller outer rings
like planets with unfledged inhabitants
whose language can't be spoken, round a sun
that spreads its light like yolk along the lawn),
duck-eggs, and seven empty pigeon shells
whose hatchlings hang arse-up along a wire.
The ceiling leans toward them like a sky
whose robin's-egg-blue arc has just one fault.
Before your outer galaxy I quail:
its compass points—ambition, comfort, luck,
a ghost, desire—are shifting on the chart.

O egging (over) of my pudding (*proof*
whereof is where? I ask). My open mouth.
O germ, O ovoid calm, O heavy world.
My love my love.
                        This rubber egg: the shtick
a child would use, to beat the laughter out.

This is Happening
for Eamonn Shanahan

    Traffic is moving, but slowly, and Hackney's acid rain,
drumming on Town Hall and children and blue-lit trees,
   creates a theatrical screen, behind which is
such action as can be mustered by this day.
   People are indistinct, as always, their vagaries
hidden from the casual observer, their actions
   uninterpretable—as when this man at the bus stop
drops his scraggy fag end into a puddle,
   when there's a bin right next to where he's standing.
It fizzes, and lies there inert. He gets on the bus,
   shaking his newspaper. Elsewhere you,
my beloved friend, read *your* newspaper
   and its pages flutter every time you blink
(as even the smallest displacement must make an impact
   on the things around it). You sip your coffee
and roll a cigarette. The lighter clicks
   and smoke drifts upwards, forming and unforming itself,
a blue beatification around your head,
   which is bent at a certain angle, and round your eyes
scanning the dry world, or at least the shadow of it
   left by ink on newsprint. Dear one,
only three days ago it was both sunny and dry
   (though it had rained in the night, and the ground was wet,
and mud was thick on the path) as our guide led us—
   a talkative Virgil—down slopes, past columns and doorways,
past a broken steeple, until we arrived
   at Plot 52512, our destination.
Along the way, five quiet Victorian angels
   had left whatever close work they were doing
and greyly, kindly, smiled as we went past.
   The stone of which they were carved was a soft,
violet-shaded stone, and they were growing
   vines on polished vines—that place is rich,
rich as a city. We stood by a stone, and your head
   was tilted at the same tilt as theirs,

as if you'd been quick to pick up the local custom.
  Somewhere below where we were, and maybe glad
to see us, if he could, through his roof of earth,
  our friend, now marked on his new body
as 'poet' and a citizen of that strange city.
  What is it we say when we're not confident
that what we're saying is important, or true?
  We say, *it's not exactly cast in stone* . . .
well this is. And it's heavy. Around it, snowdrops
  were beginning, and the earth was as soft as flesh
closing around a wound. And under, under . . .
  We loved him. Now, this morning, you're wreathed in smoke
which clings to your kitchen like the shadow of a vine
  while I watch grey and violet rivulets
pick up traffic-light colours as they fall.
  Beyond the teary windows of the bus
random elements form and unform themselves
  like the shapes behind a theatre curtain—which always,
once it's lifted, turn out to have been the stagehands
  who set the whole thing up—and the city
peels back behind me as the bus cuts through puddles,
  breaks reflections open, makes a noise
like the sound of the universe. We've never been closer.
  I'm reading a book, and in it the author has written:
This is Happening This is Happening This is Happening

The Master and the Future

Large and full and high the future still opens
And I will look radiantly forward, protected
By the great proscenium arch of the heavens.
Standing directly under its blue velvet curtain
I am separated from the past and all its broken
Props, which will now be stored backstage
And never, if I can determine it, glued together.

The future still opens full and high, and large
Like a book, the one great book you can never
Hope to stop writing in, because the one great hope
Is that one may face the future openly and without fear,
Without fear of the past, which continues to beckon,
And what it or the mooted reality of it may mean.
I have my head, thank God, full of visions.
The screen is behind me and the past is behind the screen.

Standing under the gold fringe which fringes
The blue velvet curtain, cusp of present and future,
I gaze into the faces of my as-yet-unborn audience
And in their vacant eyes I see only myself,
Which is good; which means they are for me to invent,
Beautiful as they are, and grandly as I may call to them
And however painfully they may choose to answer.

Large and high the future exquisitely opens
Over chestnut trees in full flower along a promenade
Where the park widens out to a horseshoe shape, courting
Sly clouds that dawdle over scampering puppies
And over a certain interesting girl on a young man's arm,
That roll like hoops alongside great waves of what is possible;
Opens into the chance to breathe afresh again, as if
One had never breathed the old torpid air full of mistakes:
Clicks, in fact, open like an ivory fan.
It is now indeed that I may do the work of my life.

Notes

MY DISH: The picture in my dish is a reproduction of a painting by the pre-Raphaelite painter Henry Holiday, which hangs in the Walker Art Gallery, Liverpool. Of course, it depicts the second — and last — time Dante saw Beatrice, at the age of 18. She was dead only a few years later.

COSÌ FAN TUTTE: The title means, technically, 'that's what all *women* do' — 'tutte' being the feminine form. I have stuck to the name of Mozart's opera, rather than changing it to 'tutti'. The story revolves around deception, disguise and infidelity — and the duet quoted in the poem is both very beautiful and the culmination of that.

DREAM: THE TWELVE DANCING PRINCESSES: In the fairy tale, twelve beautiful princesses wear out all their slippers every night, dancing in a murky, enchanted underworld.

THE MOOSE: The quote, 'It's not about the thing you fling, it's the fling itself', comes from one of the radio DJ character Chris in the Morning's famous monologues in the TV series *Northern Exposure*.

THE DIVE: GLOUCESTER: Oh you mighty gods!
This world I do renounce, and in your sights
Shake patiently my great affliction off...

    EDGAR: Hadst thou been aught but gossamer, feathers, air,
So many fathom down precipitating,
Thou'dst shiver'd like an egg: but thou dost breathe...
Ten masts at each make not the altitude
Which thou hast perpendicularly fell:
Thy life's a miracle. Speak yet again.
                                King Lear, Act IV, Scene VI

THE MASTER AND THE FUTURE: After the catastrophic failure in January 1895 of his only play, *Guy Domville* — on which he had pinned all his hopes — Henry James wrote in his notebook, 'Large and full and high the future still opens... It is now indeed that I may do the work of my life.'

Lightning Source UK Ltd.
Milton Keynes UK
UKOW041222221012

200974UK00001B/49/P